STRESS LESS COLORING:
PEACEFUL PATTERNS

100+ COLORING PAGES FOR CALM AND RELAXATION

Adamsmedia

Avon, Massachusetts

MW01014031

Published by
Adams Media, a division of F+W Media, Inc.
57 Littlefield Street, Avon, MA 02322. U.S.A.
www.adamsmedia.com

Contains material adapted from *The Everything® Stress Management Book* by Eve Adamson, copyright © 2002 by
F+W Media, Inc., ISBN 10: 1-58062-578-9, ISBN 13: 978-1-58062-578-4.

ISBN 10: 1-4405-9481-3
ISBN 13: 978-1-4405-9481-6

Printed in the United States of America.

10 9 8 7 6 5 4 3 2 1

Many of the designations used by manufacturers and sellers to distinguish their products are claimed as trademarks.
Where those designations appear in this book and F+W Media, Inc. was aware of a trademark claim, the designations
have been printed with initial capital letters.

This book is intended as general information only, and should not be used to diagnose or treat any health condition.
In light of the complex, individual, and specific nature of health problems, this book is not intended to replace
professional medical advice. The ideas, procedures, and suggestions in this book are intended to supplement, not
replace, the advice of a trained medical professional. Consult your physician before adopting any of the suggestions
in this book, as well as about any condition that may require diagnosis or medical attention. The author and publisher
disclaim any liability arising directly or indirectly from the use of this book.

Cover design by Stephanie Hannus.
Cover images © Hanna Saienko/123RF; Galina Nikolaeva/123RF.

This book is available at quantity discounts for bulk purchases.
For information, please call 1-800-289-0963.

INTRODUCTION

Looking to relax? Want to feel more creative? Need more peace and quiet in your life?

If you're looking to get rid of all the extra stress in your life, just pick up a pencil, crayon, or marker and let *Stress Less Coloring: Peaceful Patterns* help you manage your worries in a fun, easy, therapeutic way.

Over the years, studies have shown that coloring allows your mind to concentrate solely on the task at hand, which brings you into a restful state similar to what you can achieve through meditation. When you allow yourself to focus on the creative artwork in front of you, your mind doesn't have room for all the anxiety and stress in your life. And when your mind relaxes, your body follows, by letting go of any tension and giving you a sense of peace and well-being.

Throughout the book, you'll find more than 100 black-and-white prints depicting a variety of peaceful patterns that are just waiting to be colored in. The beauty of these prints is that you can color them in however you'd like. The most relaxing colors are cool shades such as greens, blues, and purples, but if you'd rather splash bold, bright hues like red, yellow, or orange across the page, feel free! Let your own unique palette guide your hand and personalize your pattern.

So whether you're new to art therapy or have been embracing the fun of coloring for years, it's time to stress less and find your inner calm and creativity—one peaceful print at a time.

Image © magnia/123RF

Image © magnia/123RF